HABITATS

MOUNTAINS

DAVID CUMMING

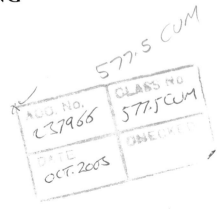
Wayland

HABITATS

Coasts   Mountains
Deserts   Polar Regions
Forests   Rivers and Lakes
Grasslands   Seas and Oceans
Islands   Wetlands

Cover: The craggy snow-topped peaks of the Rocky Mountains in Canada.
Contents page: The ibex spends much of its life high up above the snow-line of mountain ranges in Europe and northern Africa.

Series and book editor: Rosemary Ashley
Series designer: Malcolm Walker

First published in 1995 by
Wayland (Publishers) Limited
61 Western Road, Hove
East Sussex, BN3 1JD, England

British Library Cataloguing in Publication Data
Cumming, David
    Mountains. - (Habitats series)
    I. Title   II. Bull, Peter.   III. Series
    574.5264

ISBN 0-7502-1489-9

Typeset by Kudos Editorial and Design Services, England
Printed and bound in Italy by L.E.G.O. S.p.A., Vicenza

CONTENTS

1. THE WORLD'S MOUNTAINS

K2 or Mount Godwin Austen in the Himalayas. This mountain is the second highest in the world.

A mountain is steep-sided high land which is at least 300 m taller than the ground around it. A hill is high land which is below 300 m. The peak, or summit, is the name for the top of a mountain. A mountain's height is the distance between its summit and sea-level, which is usually lower than ground level. The world's highest mountain is Mount Everest, in the Himalayan range of southern Asia. Its peak is 8,848 m above sea-level.

Everest is almost certainly the highest mountain on dry land, but it is not the highest mountain on earth. This is Mauna Kea, a mountain which starts *below* sea-level and whose peak juts up through the Pacific Ocean as an island in Hawaii. From its island peak to its base on the bottom of the ocean, Mauna Kea is 10,205 m high.

An under-sea mountain is called a seamount. It is completely covered by water. The tallest under-sea mountain is a little lower than Everest, at 8,690 m high. It is situated in the Pacific Ocean, between New Zealand and Samoa.

Some mountains, like Mount Kenya in East Africa, are on their own. Most mountains, however, are part of a group or chain, called a mountain range. The most important mountain ranges in the world are the Rockies

The world's highest peaks
The world's highest peaks (fourteen, each over 8,000 m) are in the Himalayas in southern Asia. The five highest of these are listed below, followed by the five highest peaks in other mountain ranges.

Everest	*. . . . .(8,848 m)*
K2 or Godwin Austen	*. . . .(8,611 m)*
Kanchenjunga	*. . . . .(8,586 m)*
Makalu	*. . . . .(8,463 m)*
Dhaulagiri	*. . . . .(8,167 m)*
McKinley, Alaska	*. . . . .(6,194 m)*
Kilimanjaro, East Africa	*. .(5,895 m)*
Elbrus, in the Caucasus	*. . .(5,642 m)*
Aconcagua, in the Andes	*. . .(5,200 m)*
Vinson Massif, Antarctica	*.(5,140 m)*

of North America, the Andes of South America, the Alps of Europe and the Himalayas, the tallest of them all.

There are also under-sea mountain ranges whose length, width and height match all those on dry land. The Mid-Atlantic Ridge, for example, runs down the middle of the Atlantic Ocean, from near the Arctic almost to Antarctica. Its highest peaks have formed the islands of Iceland, at its northernmost point, and Bouvet, far to the south.

Mountains under threat

Mountains have always fascinated people. In early times they were regarded with reverence and awe by many people, who believed that gods lived on their summits. Strange creatures were thought to lurk on

Below This map indicates the major mountain ranges of the world.

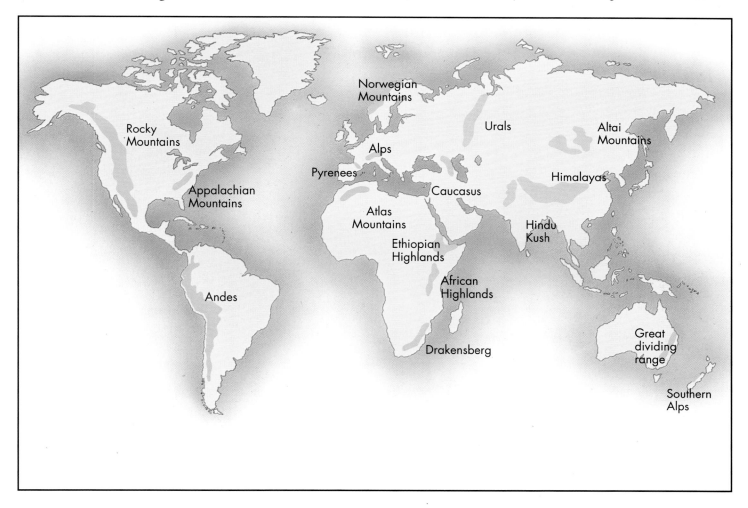

Norwegian Mountains

Rocky Mountains

Urals

Altai Mountains

Alps

Pyrenees

Himalayas

Appalachian Mountains

Caucasus

Atlas Mountains

Hindu Kush

Ethiopian Highlands

African Highlands

Andes

Drakensberg

Great dividing range

Southern Alps

the misty slopes of the mountains and among the swirling clouds at their peaks, ready to pounce on unwary travellers. Mountains have continued to hold a religious significance in many countries, and there are many myths and legends about half-human, half-animal mountain creatures.

However, most people now no longer fear to travel in mountainous areas. Mountains have been exploited for their minerals, their water power, their forests and their beautiful scenery, and the consequences of human interference have been disasterous.

Today, in many parts of the world, mountain environments are under threat after years of human abuse from farmers, foresters and increasing numbers of tourists. Mountain peoples, cultures, animals and plants have all suffered. So great has been the damage that in many parts of the world national parks have been set up to protect mountain regions. Although mountains may appear strong and enduring, they are as fragile as any other habitat and many are in danger of being ruined for ever.

The thousands of tourists who enjoy skiing on mountains all over the world are causing environmental problems.

Conquering Everest
On 29 May 1953, Edmund Hillary from New Zealand, and Tenzing Norgay from Nepal, were the first people to reach the top of Mount Everest, the highest point on earth. Since then, nearly 500 people have followed in their footsteps. Ang Rita, from Nepal, has been to the summit seven times with different expeditions. Like Tenzing Norgay, he comes from the local Sherpa mountain people. In May 1992, thirty-two people waited in line for their turn to stand on the 'roof of the world' and have their photograph taken.

Edmund Hillary took this photo of Tenzing Norgay on top of Everest.

2. HOW MOUNTAINS ARE FORMED

If you could slice the earth through the middle you would see that it has three layers: the core, the mantle and the crust. The core is in the earth's centre, about 6,400 km below the surface. Despite temperatures of 5,500 °C, the heart of the core is kept solid by the pressure of all the rocks above it. Away from the core's heart, towards the surface, the pressure decreases and the rocks become softer, melted by the high temperatures inside the earth.

The mantle, which is 3,000 km deep, is wrapped around the core. Currents of hot energy rise from the core to the top of the mantle, where they cool and then sink back, to be heated up again and rise to the top. This keeps most of the mantle semi-solid – as soft as modelling clay. However, the rocks around its rim are liquified, or molten, because there is little pressure on them and they are being heated by temperatures of 5,000 °C. This molten rim, called the asthenosphere, varies in depth from 5 km to 300 km.

The crust is around the outside of the earth. It is the layer on which we live and it 'floats' on top of the molten rim of the mantle. In relation to the rest of the earth, the crust has the thickness of the skin on an apple.

The earth's crust is divided into plates which are moving constantly. Some plates are being pushed into other plates; others are being pulled apart.

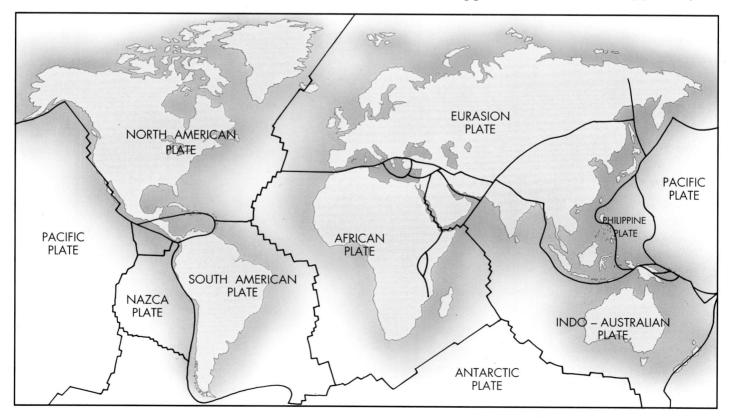

Moving plates

Unlike the skin of an apple, the crust is not a single, continuous layer of rock. It is split up into enormous slabs, called plates, which float about in the molten asthenosphere, kept moving by the currents of heat from the mantle. The plates are of two types: oceanic and continental. These names do not refer to land and water, but to different forms of the rock within the earth's crust. Oceanic plates are made of heavy, young rocks, less than 200 million years old. Continental plates contain lighter, older rocks, more than 1,500 million years old. The continental plates vary in depth from 35 km to 70 km. The oceanic plates are much thinner, only 6 km to 10 km deep in most places.

The asthenosphere's currents force neighbouring plates to move apart, to move into or just to rub against each other. It is in the areas where this action is most violent that mountains have formed, and where volcanoes and earthquakes occur. The plates move very slowly, between 1 cm to 10 cm a year, but they have been moving since the earth was created, about 4,600 million years ago.

Continental drift

About 200 million years ago the continents were joined together in a single area of land, called Pangaea (a Greek word meaning 'all-earth'), surrounded by ocean. Pangaea was like a huge jigsaw puzzle. Although locked together, its pieces were pushed and pulled by the asthenosphere's currents. Then, about 65 million years ago, the currents pulled Pangaea apart and the continents gradually drifted, over millions of years, into their present locations.

Fold mountains

Before the break-up of Pangaea, India was wedged between Africa and Asia. Following the split, the plate carrying India was pulled towards the plate

The force with which two plates collide can create fold mountains. The peaks of the folds are called 'anticlines', and the dips 'synclines'. A 'recumbent fold' is one which is forced under itself, into a double fold. Sometimes a fold breaks at a crack, or fault line, and is pushed forward. This is called a 'nappe'.

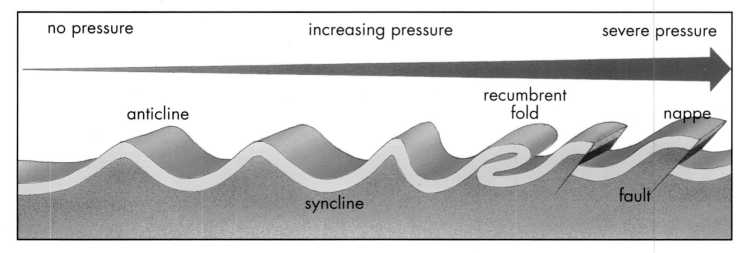

no pressure   increasing pressure   severe pressure

anticline   recumbrent fold   nappe

syncline   fault

carrying Asia. When the plates collided, the rocks in the sea-bed between them were gradually pushed up to form the Himalayan range. We know this because fossils of sea creatures have been found high up in the Himalayas.

The Rockies, Andes and European Alps were formed in a similar way – the Rockies by a collision between the North American plate and the Pacific plate, the Andes by the Nazca plate and the South American plate crashing into each other, and the Alps by the African and Eurasian plates colliding.

The Himalayas, Rockies, Andes and Alps are examples of fold mountains, the name coming from the bends, or folds, in the rock strata created when the sea-bed was squeezed between two plates. Other fold mountains include the Atlas Mountains (North Africa), the Pyrenees (between Spain and France) and the Caucasus Mountains (between the Black Sea and Caspian Sea). The folds in them can be small or up to several kilometres across.

Undersea mountains

Mountains can also be created when two plates are pulled apart. Hot, molten rock (called magma) bursts through from the asthenosphere to fill the gap in the crust. The magma piles up, cools and solidifies into mountain-high rock. The best examples of this type of mountain are on the beds of the Atlantic Ocean (the Mid-Atlantic Ridge) and Pacific Ocean (the East Pacific Rise). The Mid-Atlantic Ridge has been formed by the North and South American plates moving away from the African and Eurasian plates. Similarly, the East Pacific Rise was the result of the Pacific and Nazca plates moving apart.

An oceanic plate is forced under a continental plate. The oceanic plate melts, forming magma which rises to the earth's surface to form volcanoes.

Ocean spreading: plates move apart under the ocean and magma rises to form new ocean floor and volcanic islands.

Collision zone: where plates collide, rocks are squeezed into fold mountains. Volcanoes form in or near these mountains.

A cross-section of the earth's crust, showing how the plates are moved by currents in the mantle.

The magma produces undersea volcanoes which can grow tall enough for their peaks to be above sea-level. Surtsey (an island south of Iceland) on the Mid-Atlantic Ridge and Easter Island, on the East Pacific Rise, are examples of undersea volcanoes.

The new rock filling the crack in the centre of the Atlantic is making new crust and pushing the plates further apart, in a process called 'ocean spreading'. The Atlantic Ocean is widening in this way by 4 cm a year. However, this is not altering the size of the earth because the Pacific Ocean is shrinking.

Block mountains and rift valleys

As the earth's plates have moved about, they have caused faults (cracks) in the crust. The block of land on one side of a fault can slide down the line of the fault or be pushed up it. In either case, block mountains will be the result. Most block mountains have flat tops, not pointed peaks, because they have been formed in this way – by rocks sliding up or down and not being squeezed. The Vosges Mountains in France are examples of block mountains.

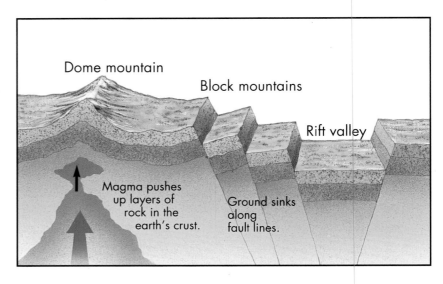

Block mountains can also be formed when two faults run parallel with each other. Again, the land in between can either be pushed up into mountains or can slip down, to leave block mountains on either side. In this case, the flat-bottomed valley between the mountains is called a rift valley, like the Great Rift Valley running through eastern Africa towards the Dead Sea, in Jordan.

Above Magma can be forced through weak points in the crust, pushing up rocks into dome mountains (see page 16). Areas of land pushed up between faults in the crust form block mountains. Rift valleys are formed when land slips down between faults.

Left Looking across the Great Rift Valley that runs through eastern Africa.

Valleys formed by erosion

Some mountain valleys have been formed by erosion – that is, rocks being worn away naturally. Pebbles, pieces of rock and boulders can tumble into a fast-flowing mountain stream. As they are swept downhill by the powerful current, they bounce and roll along the bed of the stream, gradually wearing it away and deepening it into a narrow V-shaped valley in the side of the mountain. These valleys may sometimes be widened by glaciers.

Glaciers and rivers are similar; both are water on the move, although in a glacier the water is frozen. The glacier itself moves, and it behaves more like a bulldozer than a river, eroding the land over which it travels. Rocks get trapped in the glacier's thick ice as it slips down a mountain valley. The ice becomes rough and, acting like a huge block of sandpaper, the glacier scrapes rock off the valley's floor and sides, making the floor flatter and wider, and the sides steeper. The valley loses its original V shape and becomes a deep, U-shaped valley.

Above A glacier grinding its way through the Rocky Mountains of Canada.

Along the coast of Norway there are deep inlets with high, steeply sloping sides. These are drowned valleys, called fiords, formed by glaciers in the last Ice Age (18,000 years ago). Much of northern Europe was covered in ice, which melted when temperatures rose at the end of the Ice Age. This caused the level of the sea to rise and flood the fiords along the Norwegian coast. Because they are deep, ships can sail along their full length. However, most fiords have shallow entrances, where the rocks which were pushed in front of a glacier were left when the ice melted, causing a moraine.

Right After being gouged out by a glacier, this valley filled with sea water, to become a fiord on Norway's coast.

3. VOLCANOES AND DOME MOUNTAINS

How volcanoes occur

If a continental plate hits another continental plate, both will rise up together. The Himalayas were formed in this way. However, if an oceanic plate and a continental plate collide, the oceanic plate will end up sliding under the continental plate, because it is heavier. When this happens, some of the resulting fold mountains might be volcanoes. The Rockies and Andes were created by a collision between oceanic and continental plates, so there are volcanoes in these mountain ranges – for example, Mount McKinley and Mount St Helens in the Rockies, and Cotopaxi and Chimborazo in the Andes.

As the oceanic plate slides under the continental plate, it is dragged down into the rim of the earth's mantle, the asthenosphere, where the heat melts the plate's rocks, turning them into magma. The magma is pushed to the earth's surface, erupting through the crust where weak points, like folds, have been created by the movement of plates. As we have seen with undersea mountains, volcanoes can be created by plates moving apart and magma rising to fill the gap.

> **Studying volcanoes**
> *Vulcanologists are scientists who study volcanoes. They get their name – as, indeed, do volcanoes – from Vulcan, the Roman god of fire. There are research stations on or near all active and inactive volcanoes, where vulcanologists keep an eye on what the volcano is doing. They use special instruments that can measure what is happening inside the volcano so that people have plenty of warning before an eruption.*

Cotopaxi, in Ecuador, is the highest volcano in the world. It is 5,879 m high.

Molten lava pours down the side of Mount Etna during an eruption in 1992.

Beneath the crust, molten rocks are called magma. When the magma bursts through the crust it is called lava. Lava can be thick or runny when it appears and can be accompanied by clouds of gases, ash and cinders. The hole through which all these materials appear on the earth's surface is called the crater.

Types of volcano

Most craters are at the top of the mountains (or cones) formed by volcanoes. The cones have different shapes. The commonest one – and the shape most people associate with a volcano – is a 'composite cone', like Mount Etna, on the island of Sicily, southern Italy. Its steep sides are made up of alternate layers of ash and lava. The ash is thrown out in violent eruptions, the lava in gentle eruptions.

Gases can build up beneath the cone and blow its top off, leaving behind a crater several kilometres wide. This is a called a 'caldera' volcano. Crater Lake,

Types of volcanoes
Volcanoes are classified by how often they erupt, as well as by shape. There are three types:
- *Live and active: volcanoes that erupt frequently.*
- *Live and inactive: volcanoes that erupt infrequently.*
- *Dead: volcanoes that will never erupt again.*

At the present time there are about 600 volcanoes that are considered to be live. The majority are inactive, but fifteen are active, emitting hot lava every month. Most of them are in countries around the Pacific Ocean, in an area known as the 'Ring of Fire'.

Red hot lava being blasted into the air from Kilauea, a crater on the side of Mauna Loa volcano on the island of Hawaii.

in Oregon, USA, has formed in the caldera of an extinct volcano. The Greek island of Santorini is the rim of a caldera which was flooded by the sea centuries ago.

'Shield' volcanoes, such as Mauna Loa in Hawaii, are created when the lava is very runny, so it covers a wide area before it solidifies. This type of volcano has long, gently sloping sides consisting of many layers of lava.

Sometimes, volcanoes are formed by ash and cinders building up into a cone, like Mount Paricutin in Central America.

In Iceland, there are volcanoes which have not formed cones. Iceland is part of the Mid-Atlantic Ridge, so ocean-spreading has caused cracks in the

An island is born

On 14 November 1963 some Icelandic fishermen saw bubbling and frothing in the Atlantic Ocean and great clouds of steam shooting up into the air. Although they did not know it, lava was gushing out of a crack in the Mid-Atlantic Ridge beneath them. A cone of ash 130 m tall built up, and its peak cleared the wave-tops. In April 1964, lava poured out of a hole in the peak and enclosed the ash. This quickly became solid, to form the island of Surtsey. Many other Icelandic islands have formed in this way, all because the North American and Eurasian plates are being pulled apart, causing cracks through which the asthenosphere's magma can escape.

Clouds of steam pouring from the volcano crater on Surtsey.

ground, some of which are 30 km in length. Lava has been thrown out through these cracks; it is very runny and flows great distances before it solidifies. As a result, Icelandic volcanoes have a long, low shape.

At Solfatara, near Naples in Italy, there is a volcano which has not formed a cone: its 2 km crater is little more than a hollow in the ground. The volcano is named after the sulphur gas and steam which comes out of the crater.

Like all volcanoes in Iceland, this one is low and wide.

Dome mountains

Sometimes the asthenosphere's magma does not break through the earth's crust to form a volcano. Instead, it pushes up layers of rock in the crust into a dome shape, creating dome mountains. The magma hardens into granite. When the rocks above it are worn away, the granite is exposed above the surface. The best example of dome mountains are the Black Hills in the states of South Dakota and Wyoming, in the USA. Despite their name, the Black Hills reach heights of over 2,000 m, so it is more correct to call them mountains.

Clouds of ash being blown high into the skies above Mount St Helens, in the USA, to be carried far and wide by the wind.

The effect of volcanic ash on climate

The ash thrown out by a volcano can fall up to 100 km away. It can also be thrown so high into the atmosphere that it will remain there for several years, and affect the climate of the whole earth. In 1883, the spectacular eruption of Krakatoa, in Indonesia, sent a great amount of ash into the atmosphere. Indonesia went dark for several days because the sun could not pierce the thick cloud of dust. On the other side of the world, there were stunning sunsets in the following years, which meteorologists believed were due to dust obscuring the sun's rays.

16

4. WEATHER AND CLIMATE

Several factors affect the weather and climate on mountains. The most important is altitude. The higher you climb, the colder it gets, because the air becomes thinner and cannot hold as much heat as at sea level. On average, the temperature falls 1 °C for every 150 m in altitude. This is the reason why the tops of high mountains are covered with snow and ice throughout the year, even in hot countries near the Equator – for instance Kilimanjaro and Mount Kenya in East Africa.

The snow-line is the height on a mountain above which there is always snow and ice. The snow-line varies from region to region: in cold regions it is low – for example, at the North and South Poles it is at sea-level. Around the Equator, however, it is 6,000 m above sea-level.

Because mountains are higher than the surrounding land, there is nothing to protect them, so they are very windy places, especially higher up their slopes. Strong winds also blow down the slopes. Cold air is heavy so it tends to slide down the mountainsides. The steeper the mountains, the faster this cold air will drop and the sooner strong winds will develop.

The climate on a mountain varies from one side to the other. The side facing the sun will have different weather from the side in the shade. The sunny side will be warmer. Plants that like warmth will flourish here, but not on the opposite side, which is more suited to shade-loving vegetation.

The amount of rain falling on a mountainside also depends on which way it is facing. When a mountain faces the prevailing wind (the windward side), it will be wet, while the other side (the leeward side) will be drier.

Clouds, created when warm winds cool at high altitude, drift below the summit of Mount Cook, in New Zealand's Southern Alps.

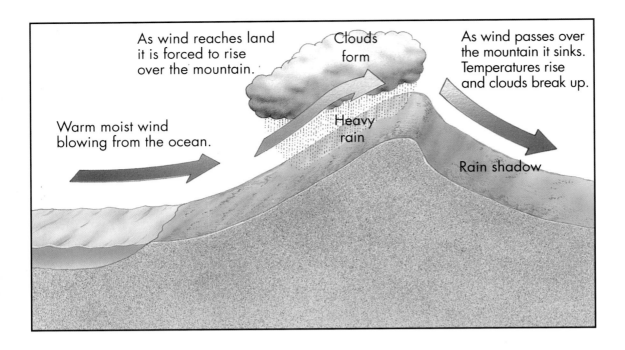

As wind reaches land it is forced to rise over the mountain.

Clouds form

As wind passes over the mountain it sinks. Temperatures rise and clouds break up.

Warm moist wind blowing from the ocean.

Heavy rain

Rain shadow

Left This diagram shows how mountainsides facing in the direction of rain-carrying winds receive most of the rainfall. Little rain falls on the other side of the mountainside, which is in the rain shadow.

Winds blowing from the ocean are warm and moisture-laden. Mountains blocking the winds' path will push them upwards. As the winds rise, they are cooled. Because cold air cannot hold as much moisture as warm air, the moisture is released, falling as rain, hail or snow on the windward side. By the time the winds descend on the leeward side of the mountain, they have lost most of their moisture, so only a little will be dropped. The leeward side is said to be in the rain shadow. The eastern sides of the Rockies, the Andes and the northern sides of the Himalayas are rain-shadow areas.

The peaks of mountains are often shrouded by clouds. The clouds consist of droplets of water formed when the warm winds cool down as they are forced up over the mountains.

Weathering

From the moment they are created, mountains start to be destroyed by wind, rain and ice, in a process called weathering. Strong winds wear away soft rocks, like limestone. These rocks are also dissolved by rain water.

Below Even though it is near the equator, Kilimanjaro is high enough to be covered with snow all year round.

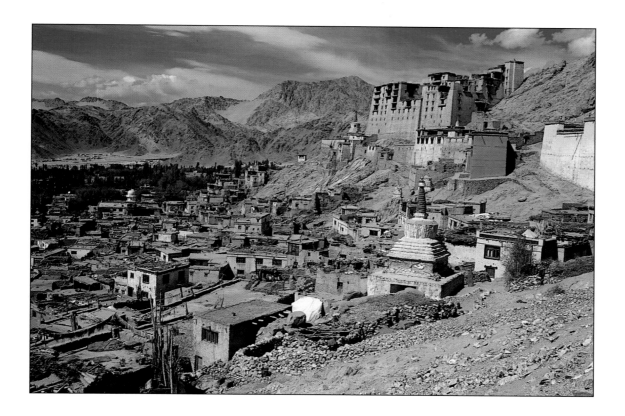

The Indian state of Ladahk suffers from dry, almost desert conditions because it lies in the rain shadow of the Himalayas.

Rainwater seeps into cracks in the rocks, where it can turn into ice. As it freezes, the water expands, widening the cracks. More water can now enter the the cracks, making them even bigger when the water freezes. Eventually, this freezing and thawing splits the rocks.

The minerals inside rocks expand in the sun's heat and contract at night. In time, this expansion and contraction will cause rocks to break apart.

Vegetation flourishes on the eastern side of the Great Dividing Range in Australia. To the west is a huge desert region caused by the rain shadow.

Australia's huge rain shadow
The Great Dividing Range (or Great Divide) runs down the eastern side of Australia. Winds blowing in from the ocean are forced to drop their rain on the eastern side of these mountains. As a result, little rain is left for the western side, which has turned into a huge desert. Little grows here, while many crops flourish to the east of the mountains, where there is plenty of rain.

5. VEGETATION

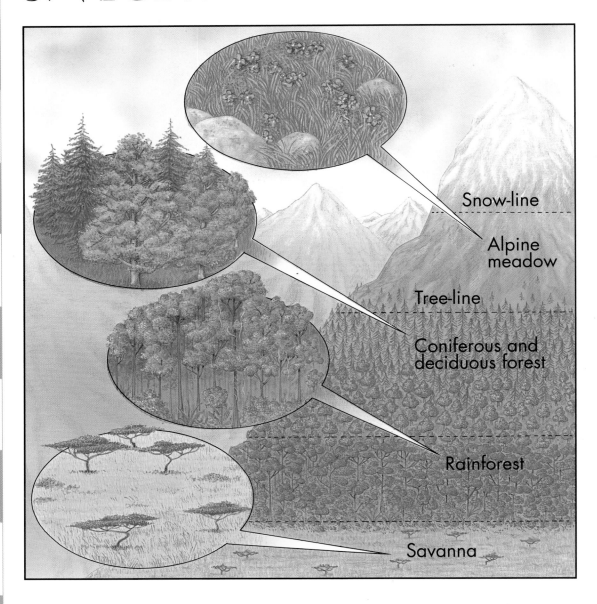

This diagram shows the different types of vegetation that can be found on a mountainside.

Snow-line

Alpine meadow

Tree-line

Coniferous and deciduous forest

Rainforest

Savanna

Mountain plants and trees have been forced to adapt in order to survive. Conditions vary with altitude. Plants and trees which like warmth, for example, will only grow near the foot of a mountain and they will not be found higher up. Mountains can be divided into vegetation zones, according to the types of trees and plants that will grow at each level on them.

Nothing grows above the snow-line because the ground is covered with snow and ice throughout the year. Below the snow-line is the treeless alpine meadow zone, where short grasses, wild flowers, mosses and lichens grow. The plants are small, with very short stems, and long roots to anchor them in the soil and prevent them being blown away by the strong winds.

In this photograph of Mount Ranier in the Rocky Mountains, we can see the alpine meadow zone just above the tree-line. Above this zone there is no vegetation, while below there are forests.

To protect them from the cold, many of these plants are covered in fine hairs. The plants have bright flowers to attract the few insects which live at this altitude.

Below the alpine meadow zone is the tree-line, which marks the highest point at which trees will grow on the mountain. The height of the tree-line is affected by climate: it is higher in hot regions than cold regions. Near the Equator, for example, the tree-line starts at 4,000 m, but in Scandinavia it is as low as 500 m.

In countries with mild climates, the tree-line will be marked by evergreen conifers – trees such as spruce, fir and pine. These trees have thick bark to protect them from the cold, and needle-like leaves on which the snow and

Left A variety of
wild flowers
blooming in the
summer sunshine
on an alpine
meadow in
southern Austria.

frost cannot settle. Below the
coniferous forests are mixed forests,
consisting of evergreen conifers and
deciduous trees such as oak and
chestnut. Finally, at the base of the
mountain, there will be only
deciduous trees.

In tropical countries, near the
Equator, the climate is too hot for
coniferous forests and the
mountainsides are covered with
rainforests or savanna.

Right A thick rainforest covers the lower
slopes of the Darren Mountains on South
Island, New Zealand.

6. WILDLIFE

The ibex, a type of wild goat, which lives in the mountains of Europe, Asia and North Africa.

Like plants and trees, mountain animals have adapted to live in their particular habitat. To keep out the cold and wind, many animals have thicker and shaggier coats than animals living in lowland regions. The hooves of sheep and goats are hard and pointed to enable them to get a good grip on steep, slippery slopes. The internal organs of mountain animals may also differ from those of lowland animals. Many have developed larger hearts and lungs to cope with the thin air at high altitudes. Yaks, a type of cattle, are so well-equipped for mountain life that herds of them happily graze in the Himalayas at heights of 6,000 m, in temperatures of -40 °C.

Animals do not live above the alpine meadow zone. They spend the summers up there, and move down in the autumn to escape the cold winters. However, some small mammals, such as snow hares and marmots, hibernate in the alpine meadow zone in winter after building up layers of fat during summer. These small mammals, as well as

Pyrenean bears
The Pyrenean brown bear, 2 m tall and weighing 200 kg, was described in the fourteenth century as a 'most common beast'. Since then, thousands have been killed, until by 1937, only 200 were left. Today, about ten still survive. These few bears roam the forested slopes of the Pyrenees Mountains between Spain and France. Although hunting them has been forbidden for many years, local shepherds continue to shoot the bears because they eat their sheep. Recently it has been agreed that shepherds will receive £150 for every sheep killed by a bear in return for not hunting them. It is also planned to extend the Pyrenean National Park so that the bears can live in safety under the watchful eyes of the park rangers.

goats and sheep, can be seen nibbling the meadows' grasses and plants. Carnivores (meat-eaters), such as wolves and pumas – and in the Himalayas, the elusive and rare snow leopard – may lurk among the rocky outcrops, ready to pounce on a grazing sheep. These creatures prefer to spend most of their time in the forests below the tree-line, where prey is more plentiful.

Mountain wildlife is most abundant in the forests on the lower slopes, especially in tropical countries, where many different types of monkeys, birds, insects and snakes can be found.

The marmot's thick fur protects it from the cold at high altitudes.

The yeti – fact or fiction?

According to legend, the yeti is a huge, ape-like creature that lives high up in the Himalayas, feeding off yaks. Some local people say the yeti is more like a human than an ape and they have nicknamed it the 'abominable snowman'. Many people claim to have seen the yeti: few scientists, however, are convinced that it exists. Perhaps they are wrong …?

24

Mountain birds

The golden eagle is one of the largest and most common birds in the skies above all the world's mountain ranges. Powerfully built to survive this high-altitude habitat, it can easily cope with the strong gusts of wind and swirling air currents found among the peaks. Up to 1.2 m long and 7 kg in weight, with a wingspan of 2.1 m, the golden eagle circles and soars, scanning the ground for prey with eyes ten times sharper than ours. Small mammals, like mountain hares, are its favourite food, and if these are in short supply, the golden eagle pounces on smaller mountain birds. Once it has spotted its victim, an eagle dives at 144 kph to grab the prey with its talons, before taking it away to a quiet spot to tear it apart with its great hooked beak.

Even larger than the golden eagle are the Californian and Andean condors. Each species measures up to 1.3 m long and 10 kg in weight. The Californian condor is one of the world's rarest birds – decades of hunting and trapping have nearly wiped out this species. The only hope for the survival of the species lay in catching and keeping the remaining birds in captivity where they can breed in safety. It is planned to start releasing some of them into the wild soon, in areas where rangers can keep a careful watch on them. The Andean condor, with a wing span of 3 m, soars above the high peaks of the Andes, ranging from the mountains to the Pacific coast. It feeds on dead animals including huge quantities of fish.

A condor gliding among the peaks of the Andes Mountains in South America.

A bald eagle flying high above the Rockies, in the USA.

The bald eagle
This is a very large type of sea eagle, measuring about 1 m in length. Bald eagles have high arched beaks and bare legs. They are found only in North America and have become the national emblem of the USA. They feed on fish from rivers and lakes, and are often found in mountainous regions of North America. Bald eagles were once hunted and killed in their thousands, especially in Alaska, where they caused problems for fishermen because they ate all the salmon.

7. MOUNTAIN PEOPLE

In the same way that plants and animals have adapted to their mountain habitats, so have mountain people. Lowland visitors to mountains above 3,000 m often suffer from 'altitude sickness' – breathlessness, light-headedness and headaches. This is because the air, being thinner, contains less oxygen: above 3,000 m, people take in with each breath about half the amount of oxygen that they take in at sea-level. Mountain peoples, such as the Sherpas of Nepal and the Aymara Indians of South America do not suffer from altitude sickness. This is because they have larger lungs to take in more oxygen, more blood cells to carry the oxygen and larger hearts to pump the blood quickly round their bodies, than people living in the lowlands.

Because mountain air is thin, more of the sun's harmful rays can pass through it. As a result, many mountain peoples have developed tough, dark skin which is not easily burnt by the sun. Fair-skinned lowlanders need sunscreen creams to protect them from sunburn when they come to the mountains.

These Sherpa women of Nepal cannot afford animals, so they have to carry everything themselves.

These Aymara women live in the Andes Mountains. They earn little money from farming so they make clothes to sell in the markets.

A tough life

Mountain people are usually among the poorest of the population in most countries. It is not easy to build roads and railways in mountainous areas, so communication is often difficult for many mountain people, who are frequently cut off from the rest of their country. As a result, some mountain communities have been almost forgotten by their government, which may give them very little support and assistance.

Cut off from the rest of India by the Himalayas, the state of Ladakh has had little assistance from the Indian government in providing modern facilities.

A mountain civilization

Most of the world's oldest civilizations developed on the plains, where life was easier than in the mountains. The Incas, a mountain people of South America, were the exception. Their great empire lasted from AD 1100 to the 1500s and it was ruled from Cuzco (in modern-day Peru), 3,500 m up in the Andes Mountains. Another important Inca city was Machu Picchu, which was built at a height of 2,400 m in the Andes.

Machu Picchu, once an important city of the Inca Empire.

While lowland areas have progressed, mountain towns and villages have usually developed more slowly. They have been the last places to get electricity, telephones, television, clean drinking water, new schools, hospitals and factories. In mountain communities in developing countries, there are usually fewer facilities and less job opportunities than in the lowlands. In the mountain regions of India and in Nepal, for example, many men are forced to leave their villages to earn money in the lowlands. Some of them join the army and send most of their earnings home. In their absence, family farms are run by the men's parents, wives and children. The men try to take their holidays at busy times of the year, such as when their crops need harvesting.

In addition to these problems, mountain people have to cope with a harsh climate. Daily life is a struggle, which has made them much hardier than lowlanders. Often isolated, and ignored by their governments, they have become independent, resourceful people who can look after themselves.

The people in this Nepalese village have stripped the land of all its trees, so the soil will soon become eroded.

The Gurkha people of Nepal, for example, have served as soldiers in the British Army for many years. They have impressed everyone with their resourcefulness, stamina and fighting skills. Similarly, the Pathan peoples, who live in the mountains of north-west Pakistan, have always provoked fear and dread in their enemies. Even today, the government of Pakistan allows the Pathans to run their own affairs and does not risk offending them by passing laws which they would not approve.

The Afghan guerrilla troops from the mountains of Afghanistan were the toughest fighters in the war between Afghanistan and the Soviet Union, which was fought in the 1980s.

The effects of deforestation on people

Mountain people often have large families. They need their children to help with farming or to earn money by going out to work. There is often a poor standard of health care in mountain communities, leading to a high death rate among children. This is another reason why mountain people have large families. In one mountain country, Nepal, the population has increased more than four times in the last forty years. To feed all these people, more farming land has been provided by cutting down trees and clearing huge areas of forest. This is called deforestation. People have also cut down trees and sold the wood for fuel. In the 1940s, 60 per cent of Nepal was covered with forests; today only 30 per cent of the land is forest.

Deforestation has affected the people in many ways. Trees protect the soil from heavy rain and their roots help to hold the soil and stop it from being washed away. The cutting down of the forests means that the already poor mountain soil is washed off the land and drains into rivers, blocking them and causing flooding.

An Indian holy man among the forests of the Himalayas.

Mountains and religion

Mountains have always been quiet, peaceful places – perfect for holy people who do not want to be troubled by the hustle and bustle of daily life. Ancient peoples believed that the mountains were the home of their gods. The ancient Greeks, for example, believed their gods lived on top of Mount Olympus, in Greece. According to the Hindu holy books, Hindu gods live in the Himalayas, and one of the most sacred rivers in India, the Ganges (or Ganga) rises there. Thousands of modern-day Hindus make pilgrimages to shrines in the Himalayas. In the Mount Athos area of northern Greece, monks have built twenty monasteries in the mountains and the only way to reach many of them is to be hauled up in a large basket.

8. FARMING

Without terraces, these Himalayan farmers would have no flat land on which to grow crops.

Most mountain people live by farming. The majority of them are subsistence farmers. This means that their farms can produce enough food for the family, but little is left over for sale in a market. Even if they have surplus food, the isolation of their farms makes it difficult for them to get their produce to market.

In many countries, mountain farmers have levelled the land by building steps, or terraces, up the slopes of the mountains. They edge the terraces with stone walls, which help to prevent the rain washing away the soil.

Left Farmers in the Andes Mountains of South America breed llamas for their wool.

Mountain soil is poor for growing crops because it is thin and stony. Crops grown in mountain areas include cereals, fruit and vegetables in temperate countries, and coffee and bananas in tropical lands.

Except in developed countries, few mountain farmers have money to buy machines or even good-quality tools, so most of the work is done by hand, with animals being used to pull ploughs and carts. Even in developed countries, the slopes are often so steep that the farmers can only use the smallest machines.

The rearing of animals is an important feature of mountain farming. In temperate mountain regions such as the European Alps, the mountains of Scandinavia and the Rockies of North America, the livestock reared is mainly

dairy cattle, sheep and goats. In winter, the animals are kept on the lower slopes, housed in barns during the coldest periods. In summer, farmers may take their animals up to graze on the nourishing grasses and plants of the alpine meadows. Sometimes the farmer will be accompanied up the slopes by his whole family, who will spend the summer in their mountain home. They will harvest the dried grass (hay) to feed the animals in winter and

Below This Himalayan farmer uses a type of yak called a dzo to pull his plough.

In summer, the hay is cut and cattle are grazed in these alpine meadows in Switzerland. In winter, the meadows are buried beneath thick snow.

may make dairy products, including butter and cheese. In the autumn, the family and animals return to the lower slopes, where they will spend the winter. This annual movement of farmers and animals is called transhumance.

In other mountain regions different animals are reared, such as yaks in the Himalayas and llamas in the Andes of South America. These animals are used for carrying goods, pulling farm equipment and providing meat and milk for food, or wool and hides for clothing.

Many uses of a yak

Some mountain animals have been domesticated by farmers. A yak, for instance, can be used for:

- *pulling a plough*
- *carrying heavy loads*
- *providing milk for drinking and making into butter*
- *providing skins for clothes, blankets and floor rugs*
- *providing dung, which can be used as a fertilizer and as fuel.*

This team of yaks in Nepal is being used for carrying people and equipment on a climbing expedition.

9. INDUSTRY, TOURISM AND POWER

Mines and quarries

Most mountain ranges have been formed by enormous upheavals in the earth's crust. Their rocks have experienced terrific pressures and high temperatures which have changed them. For example, soft limestone has been squeezed into hard marble, and crumbly shales (fine rocks) into brittle slate. Italy's Apennine Mountains are famous for the quarries where marble has been removed for centuries. The marble is used in buildings and for sculptures.

During the formation of mountains, hot, molten magma from the asthenosphere has oozed up into the rocks to settle in the gaps and cracks between them. Here the magma has cooled into 'veins' of useful or rare minerals. Valuable gold, silver and platinum may be found. However, most of the minerals are mixed with others to form mineral ores, such as iron ore and zinc ore. Mines are dug into the mountainsides so that

A copper mine in the mountains of Mexico.

The lure of gold

Mountain streams often flow over veins of mineral ores and wash tiny pieces of them down to the plains. The discovery of gold in streams from the Rockies led to 'gold rushes' in North America at the end of the nineteenth century. One of the most famous was the Klondyke Gold Rush, to the Klondyke River in the Yukon, north-west Canada, in 1896–98. Thousands of gold prospectors left their homes and travelled huge distances in the hope of making their fortunes. Few became rich; many died. Today, ghost towns are all that remain of these exciting times.

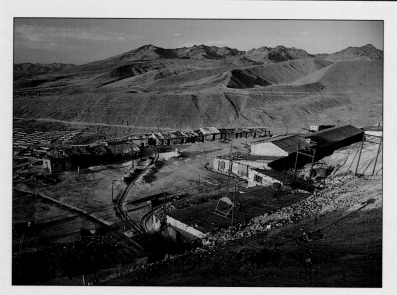

A mountain of silver

Potosi is a small town 4,000 m up in the Andes Mountains in Bolivia, South America. It was built at the foot of the 800-m-high Cerro Rico (the Rich Mountain), so named because it was full of silver ore. In the 1500s, Spanish conquistadores (conquerors) discovered the mountain when they invaded the region now called Bolivia and brought it into the Spanish Empire. By the end of the eighteenth century, huge amounts of silver had been taken and the Spaniards left Potosi, believing that they had removed all the mountain's silver.

Some 10,000 miners now work in the 500 tunnels dug into Cerro Rico. It is dangerous work and they earn low wages because only low-quality silver ore remains.

The entrance to one of the ancient silver mines founded by the Spaniards. Here miners still dig for silver, deep in the Cerro Rico mountain in Bolivia.

these riches can be extracted. Sometimes the ores lie close to the surface and there is no need for digging deep into the ground, so the mines are open-cast.

Forestry

In some mountain regions forestry is an important industry. On the slopes of the Rocky Mountains in the USA and Canada are softwoods, such as spruce, pine and aspen, which are used for building. In the Appalachian Mountains, in the eastern USA, there are hardwood forests, where timber is cut down and used for many purposes.

Many countries now limit the number of trees that can be cut down for their timber.

Valuable hardwood trees such as teak, mahogany and ebony grow in mountain forests in many tropical regions of the world. Timber may be taken from these forests, but in many countries it is against the law to cut down trees in mountainous regions because of mudslides and other damage resulting from the loss of forests.

Tourism

In almost all mountainous areas the most valuable resource does not lie below the ground, but on top of it. This is the landscape itself. Tourism is now one of the most important industries in mountain regions. People come from far and wide to enjoy the often spectacular scenery, breathe in the clean air and take part in pastimes and sports, ranging from relaxing walking and sightseeing to more energetic activities like skiing, climbing and mountain biking.

To cater for all their needs, hotels, restaurants, cable cars, shops and ski-lifts have to be built, and people employed to operate them. Tourism brings jobs into an area where they are hard to find. The jobs are usually all-year round, since many people visit the mountains in the summer as well as in the winter. There is plenty to do there at all times of the year.

Above Rock climbing is a very popular mountain sport in the summer months when the snow has melted.

Right A team of mountain walkers enjoying the clean air and beautiful scenery.

However, tourism can be very damaging to mountain areas. Walkers and bikers, for example, wear away paths and leave rubbish. In Nepal, it is said that you do not need a map to get to Everest: just follow the trail of drink cans and sweet wrappers left by others. Tourists in Nepal have contributed to the deforestation of the Himalayas. Many people go hiking in the hills and mountains and stay at guest houses owned by local people. As the number of visitors increase, the more wood the locals need for fuel for cooking and heating, so more trees are chopped down. Trees are also needed for building guest houses and other facilities for tourists.

In isolated mountain regions, tourists can bring disease, or they may introduce customs which disturb the local people's traditional way of life – for example, when tourists wear shorts or bikinis where the local people are Muslim, and believe the body should be covered.

Skiing is an important part of the winter tourist industry in the French Alps.

Hydroelectric power

Falling water produces power which can be used to turn turbines, connected to generators, to make electricity. Mountain rivers are ideal for generating hydroelectricity because they are very powerful as they thunder down the steep slopes to the plains. Dams containing turbines can be built across these rivers to make use of their power. Dams can also be built across rivers in mountain valleys, so that reservoirs (artificial lakes) build up behind them.

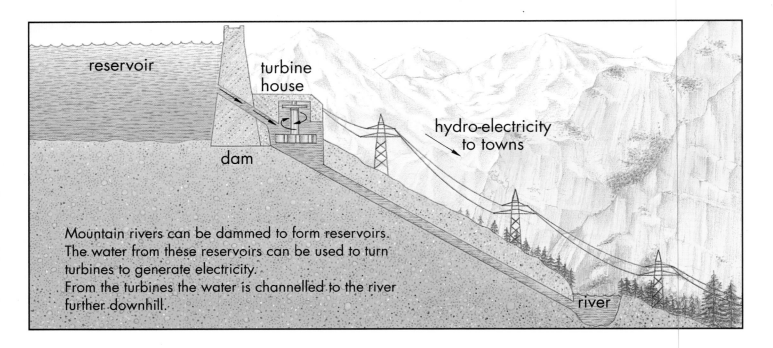

reservoir

turbine house

dam

hydro-electricity to towns

Mountain rivers can be dammed to form reservoirs. The water from these reservoirs can be used to turn turbines to generate electricity. From the turbines the water is channelled to the river further downhill.

river

When the water empties out of the reservoir, it can be used to drive turbines. Mountainous countries like Switzerland and Norway generate most of their electricity in this way.

Dams and hydroelectric power stations are costly, but once they have been built, they produce electricity very cheaply. This is an environmentally friendly way of making electricity because no harmful fossil fuels are involved. However, if a reservoir has to be created, then the environment is affected because thousands of hectares of land are flooded by its waters, perhaps causing farms or even villages to be moved, and destroying the habitat for wildlife.

This diagram shows how the power of falling water can be used to generate hydroelectricity.

Using the Snowy River

The Snowy River flows down the eastern side of the Great Dividing Range in Australia. Its fast-flowing waters are being used for hydroelectricity and for irrigation. Sixteen dams and nine power stations have been built on the river. In addition, 160 km of pipes divert river water to irrigate farms situated in the rain shadow on the west of the mountains. This region was previously too dry for growing crops but now, with irrigation, they can be planted.

One of the dams used in a hydroelectricity scheme on the Snowy River, in Australia.

10. TRANSPORT PROBLEMS

In the past mountains formed a barrier for people. They could only be crossed by travelling through the passes between valleys. The passes could be used in summer, but not in winter, when they were often blocked by deep snow and the paths leading up to them were treacherous with ice. Even if the passes were free from snow in winter, bitterly cold temperatures made travel across them impossible.

Nowadays, in developed countries, mountains are no longer great obstacles to travel, although some high passes can still be closed in winter. Planes and helicopters can fly over even the highest mountains. Long tunnels for trains and vehicles have been cut through many mountain barriers, such as the Simplon and St Gotthard Tunnels in the Alps. Roads zigzag up one side of mountain ranges and down the other, for example the Karakoram Highway through the Karakoram mountain range, leading from Pakistan into China.

This tunnel through the Alps makes it easier to travel between Switzerland and Italy.

Most developing countries, however, do not have the money to build transport routes through mountainous areas. Often there are no roads, only tracks, just wide enough for a horse or donkey to struggle up, laden with food or firewood. Sometimes there are only footpaths which are too narrow even for animals. People have to carry heavy sacks of grain or water containers on their backs to take to their homes.

Landslides and avalanches

Landslides frequently occur on mountains. On steep slopes, rocks and soil may be loosened by heavy rain and wind and sent crashing downhill. Roads can be blocked and villages cut off for weeks while all the material is cleared away. Deforestation makes the problem worse because the soil is washed off the mountainsides more easily by heavy rain. In 1920 there was a terrible landslide in China which killed at least 180,000 people.

Above The Karakoram highway zizags over the Karakoram mountains, part of the Himalayan range, allowing vehicles to travel from China into Pakistan.

Left A large mass of snow pours down a mountainside in the French Alps. Avalanches are a constant threat to people and property in mountainous areas.

Mountain porters crossing a stream in the Himalayas. In a treacherous place like this, humans are more reliable than animals.

Landslides are sometimes caused by earthquakes, which are common in mountainous areas. As we have already seen, mountains have formed in places where the crust's plates are moving. As they bump and grind against each other, vibrations may be sent through the layers of rock, causing the ground above to shake. The shaking may dislodge huge chunks of mountainside, sending it tumbling into the valley below.

In winter, communications in mountain areas can be disrupted by avalanches, which close roads and destroy telephone lines. An avalanche is a large mass of snow which slips down a mountainside, knocking over and burying everything in its way. Avalanches are started by vibrations – these may be caused by an earthquake or earth tremor, or even a loud noise, like a gunshot or shouting. In areas where avalanches occur often, strong fences are built and forests planted to try to slow them and shorten the distance of their path.

Truck pollution in Switzerland

In February 1994, the people of Switzerland voted against foreign trucks travelling across their country. Gases from truck exhausts are one reason for acid rain, which has killed an alarming number of trees on Swiss mountainsides. Without the trees' roots to hold it together, the soil slides down the slopes more easily and causes damage to villages. The Swiss government plans to build two new rail tunnels through the Alps, which will allow trains to transport 3 million trucks a year across Switzerland, so that they will not need to use the country's roads.

11. CONSERVATION FOR THE FUTURE

Mountains under threat

Tall and mighty, mountains certainly do not appear weak and easily damaged. In fact, as we have seen, they are readily harmed and continue to be under constant attack from nature and from humans.

Beneath the earth's crust, strong currents within the asthenosphere continue to move the plates, which can lead to earthquakes. Then, huge chunks of mountainside may be dislodged and disappear into the valleys.

Taller than the surrounding land, mountains are unprotected from the worst of the weather. They receive the full force of wind and rain, both of which wear away the mountain's rocky exterior. The Himalayas, for example, are among the world's youngest mountains. Their rocks are still relatively 'soft' compared with those on older mountains. In every square kilometre, 1,000 tonnes of rock are being worn away each year.

Although Mount Everest, the world's highest mountain, looks strong and enduring, it is actually quite soft and easily eroded by the weather.

Humans are adding to the destruction of the Himalayas, which were once covered with forests on their lower slopes. Today, many of the mountainsides in developing countries are bare, their trees chopped down for fuel, for building materials and for making furniture. The grass on many of their pastures is very thin, because too many goats and sheep have been allowed to graze on them without giving the grass enough time to grow. The roots of the trees and grass helped prevent the soil being blown away by the wind and washed downhill by the rain. Without their protection, a lot of soil is being lost every year. As the soils become thin and poor, farmers start cutting down more trees to sell because they cannot earn anything from their land. And so the damage continues – and worsens.

In many wealthy mountain countries, human pollution – from industry and car and truck exhausts – is causing the acid rain which is destroying whole forests.

Little will grow on this deforested hillside in India because the soil is now very thin and stony.

People are also harming the mountains by visiting them. Tourists are wearing away paths, uprooting plants, frightening the wildlife and leaving behind rubbish which is non-biodegradable. This is even a problem on Mount Everest because many big expeditions come to climb it every year. Now, climbers have to bring down everything they take up – unless it is biodegradable, in which case it can be buried to rot away.

Tourism is also encouraging people to abandon farm work. Many farmers' children prefer to work in hotels, restaurants or shops, where they can earn more money than from farming. As a result, mountain land is neglected and becomes ruined.

Some conservation solutions

Of course, nothing can be done to stop nature's destruction of mountains. Humans, however, can reduce the amount of harm they do to them.

Already, many countries have opened special mountain parks, where humans interfere as little as possible with the landscape and animals. Rangers keep a careful eye on people's behaviour to ensure that they abide by the rules. They can make visitors pay large fines if they catch them disturbing the animals or dropping rubbish.

In developing countries, government officials are being trained to visit mountain villages to give advice on improving farming methods. They advise against over-grazing pastureland and are also encouraging families to open handicraft workshops to earn money, as an alternative to cutting down trees. The governments themselves are trying to spend more money in mountain areas so that there are better facilities for the local people, in the hope that fewer will move away to the lowlands or to work in the tourist industry.

Many developing countries are unsure about tourism. On the one hand it brings them much-needed money and provides many jobs. On the other hand it can do a lot of harm – not only to the environment, but to local ways of life and cultures. The small Himalayan kingdom

Above Much of this rubbish in the Himalayas has been dropped by tourists.

Some of the unspoilt forests of the Himalayan Kingdom of Bhutan, which it is feared could be destroyed by tourism.

of Bhutan has decided that tourism does more harm than good. Only a few foreigners are allowed to visit the country each year, and they have to pay a large fee before they are allowed in. In this way, Bhutan earns a lot of money from a few tourists. Bhutan's neighbour, Nepal, however, does not limit the number of tourists allowed in and thousands of people go there every year to walk along its mountain paths. The tourists have to buy a special permit to do this and the money is used to clear up the mess made by walkers and to repair the damage done to paths by all their boots. However, Nepal tries to restrict the number of climbers on Mount Everest by charging them a very high fee for permission to climb the mountain. Every climbing expedition has to pay US$10,000 per person.

   All over the world, in both developed and developing countries, there is a growing awareness of the need to protect mountain areas so that future generations can enjoy them as much as we do at present.

Mount McKinley, the highest mountain in North America, photographed from Denali National Park in Alaska. Great care is taken in national parks such as this, to ensure that the beautiful scenery is not harmed by tourists.

GLOSSARY

Acid rain   Rain that contains poisonous chemicals, absorbed from factory smoke and traffic exhaust fumes.

Alpine   Relating to high mountains.

Altitude   The height above sea-level.

Conifers   Evergreen trees with cones.

Conservationists   People who try to protect the environment from being harmed.

Core   The centre of the earth.

Crust   The outside of the earth, on which we live.

Deciduous trees   Trees which lose their leaves in winter.

Deforestation   The cutting down and clearance of trees from land.

Elusive   Shy, difficult to see or catch.

Environment   The surroundings in which humans, animals and plants live.

Evergreen trees   Trees which keep their leaves all year.

Exploitation   To use up resources without thinking about the consequences.

Extinct   No longer active.

Fossils   The remains or traces of animals found preserved in rock.

Fossil fuels   Naturally occurring fuels, such as coal, oil, peat and natural gas, which have been formed by the decaying of organic matter.

Foothills   The smaller hills along the edge of a mountain range.

Habitat   The place where a species of animal or plant lives naturally.

Hibernate   To spend the winter in a deep sleep.

Hydroelectricity   Electricity generated by the power of falling water.

Ice Age   A period in history when much of the earth was covered with ice. The last Ice Age was about 18,000 years ago.

Irrigation   Supplying farming land with water through canals, channels and pumps.

Lava   Molten rock from the mantle that comes out of cracks in the earth's crust.

Magma   Molten rocks beneath the earth's crust.

Mantle   The layer between the earth's crust and core.

Minerals   Naturally-occuring substances in rocks and soil.

Molten   Liquid, melted by high temperatures.

Moraine   A mass of debris such as soil and rocks, carried by a glacier and forming ridges and mounds when it is deposited.

National parks   Areas of countryside in which the wildlife and scenery is protected from harm.

Non-biodegradable   Something that does not rot naturally.

Open-cast mining   Mining by digging down from the surface rather than tunnelling underground.

Pass   Low land between mountains which people use to travel through mountainous areas.

Plates   Large sections of the earth's crust which move about.

Persecution   Attacking a person for their religious beliefs.

Prevailing wind   The direction from which a wind usually comes.

Reservoir   A lake created by a dam across a river.

Soviet Union   A former group of republics in Eastern Europe and Western Asia which broke up into separate states in 1991.

Strata   Layers of rocks.

Species   A group of animals or plants that are very similar or related.

BOOKS TO READ AND FURTHER INFORMATION

The *National Geographic* and *Geographical* magazines often have interesting articles about mountain areas.

Mountains by Brian Knapp (Simon Schuster, 1989)
Mountains by Tom Mariner (Cherrytree, 1989)
Mountains by Terry Jennings (Oxford University Press, 1986)
The Alps and their People by Sue Bullen (Wayland, 1994)
The Mountain by Lionel Bender (Franklin Watts, 1988)
Tibetans by Judith Kendra (Wayland, 1993)
Volcano by John Dudman (Wayland, 1993)

For information about mountains in various countries you could contact the following organizations:

British Mountaineering Council
Crawford House
Precinct Street
Booth Street East
Manchester M13 9RZ.

For more information about wildlife under threat, you could contact the following organizations:

Friends of the Earth (UK)
26-28 Underwood Street
London N1 7JQ.

Worldwide Fund for Nature
Panda House
Weyside Park
Godalming
Surrey GU7 1XR

Picture acknowledgements
Britstock-IFA cover,/Tetsuo Sayama 17(lower); David Cumming 19(top), 27(lower), 30, 32(lower); Eye Ubiquitous /L.Fordyce 11(top), 21(top), /J.B.Pickering 39, /D.Cumming 40, /J.Waterlow 41(top); Hutchison Library 27(top), J.Horner 35(top); Frank Lane Picture Agency /Silvestris iii & 23, /L.Lee Rue 24(top), /C.Mullen 31, /T.Wharton 33; NHPA /B.Hawkes 15(top), /J.Meech 22(lower), /J.Shaw 35(lower), /38, /N.A. Callow 41(lower); Royal Geographical Society 6(lower), Still Pictures /M. Edwards 5, /R.Van der Giessen 12, /D.Decobecq 13, /M.& C.Denis Huot 17(top), /Udo Hirsch 28, /J.Etchart 29, 32(top), /45; Tony Stone Worldwide /J.Noble 4, /R.Elliot 6(top), A.Husmo ii 11(lower), G.Vaughan 14, /B.Parsley 15(lower), /S.Huber 22(top), /D.J.Cox 24(centre), C.Prior 26, /L.Lefkowitz 34, /J.McBride 36(top), /D.Smetzer 36(lower), /N.DeVore 42, /44(top), Topham Picture Source 10 (lower), 16, 37, 43; Zefa /Armstrong 16.
Artwork on pages 5, 7, 8, 9, 10, 18 by Peter Bull, and on pages 20 and 38 by John Yates.

INDEX

Numbers in **bold** refer to photographs.